# CIAO, BABY

ESSENTIAL POETS SERIES 97

Guernica Editions acknowledge the financial support
of the Canada Council for the Arts.

Canadä

Guernica Editions acknowledge the financial support of the
Government of Canada through the Book Publishing Industry
Development Program (BDIPD).

GIANNA PATRIARCA

# CIAO, BABY

GUERNICA
TORONTO·BUFFALO·LANCASTER (U.K.)
1999

Antonio D'Alfonso, editor
Guernica Editions Inc.
P.O. Box 117, Station P, Toronto (ON), Canada M5S 2S6
2250 Military Road, Tonawanda, N.Y. 14150-6000 U.S.A.
Gazelle, Falcon House, Queen Square, Lancaster LA1 1RN
U.K.

Printed in Canada.

Legal Deposit — Fourth Quarter
National Library of Canada
Library of Congress Catalog Card Number: 99-64480
Canadian Cataloguing in Publication Data
Ciao, baby
(Essential poets series ; 97
Poems.
ISBN 1-55071-096-6
I. Title. II. Series.
PS8581.A6665C52  1999  C811'.54 C99-900871-4
PR9199.3.P344C52  1999

# Contents

For Gia, Luciana, Francesca and Mauro,
i give you the real-estate of my heart

Per Arduino,
il mio cuore senza passaporto

*Remember how we picked the daffodils?*
*Nobody else remembers, but I remember.*

Ted Hughes

# Simple Heart

i will not write epics
to anthologize
sometimes ideas hurt my head
they take me places where
i am not comfortable
where i am always a stranger

but i will write about you
and the gentleness you are
inside my arms
the scent you bring
with your morning eyes
all the possibilities
there in the almond shapes
beneath your brows

i will write about the
treasure you are in your
dollar t-shirt and
hand me down jeans
you make all the ideas
take a second seat
there is too much of me
you want
there is too much of me
you need
and i am yours

i will find my dreams again
because of you

my tender string bean
who grows so tall
so quickly
i must keep the muscles moving
i must exercise the knees
keep on walking to meet you
halfway wherever we are going

take my hand, my heart
they have been yours from
the very first breath
they will be yours
long after all the ideas
have been explored

# My English Love

that i am loved at all
surprises me
that i am loved by you
mystifies me

but it is twenty years
from that summer night
beneath a Sunday moon
on holiday
fat and golden against
a huge Canadian sky

such a foreign face
such a timid smile
and good evening
never sounded so musical

that you stood
as i began to sit
was charming
that you spoke my name
*Giovanna*
without mistake
suddenly it was the right name
each vowel and consonat perfect
it was always the right name
waiting for the sound you were
and my heart began to re-arrange
its history
making room for you

that i have not written you
love poems in twenty years
is a mystery
but perhaps poets only
write about what is missing

# The First House

Aldergrove Avenue
was a dead end street
by the railway tracks
a multicultural street
long before the government
made it policy

Brenda and Ross lived there
they were white trash
so my uncle said
garbage people he called them
Rosemary and Michal were Irish
and Mrs. Bailey lived in the little
house with six cats
but Georgina Pappadimitrou
was my first Canadian friend
a tall gangly girl
with lips so thin
they seemed a cut on her face
her hair was long and black
thick as a horse's tail
she was thirteen and i was ten
but we were equal
except she had brothers
and i had none
Georgina cooked and cleaned
like my mother did
but late at night
when it was dark and still
she'd throw pebbles at my

basement window
we would sneak out
behind the railroad tracks
and smoke Export A's
she'd stolen from her brothers
we would stare at the sparse
distant stars and she would
tell me about a town by an ocean
i would tell her about a town
at the bottom of hills
the cigarette smoke rising softly
into the Canadian sky
we counted the trains into the night
wondering which one was going
to the ocean and which one was
going someplace else

☆

Brenda and Ross loved
to torture me
up the Woodbine hill
just before Danforth Avenue
they waited for me each
afternoon on my way home
from Gledhill Public
each day like a blessed penance
the litany in chorus
"fat wop, fat wop, where ya
going, you fat wop"
and the stones whipped by me
at times stinging my legs
drumming my back
and i ran, i ran

as fast as my fat legs
could carry me
up the thirty odd steps
to Aldergrove
ran with the sting in my
eyes and my flesh
like a stunned, stupid rabbit
never once thinking
of picking up a stone
and throwing it back

☆

uncle Jake had built his
semi-detached, brick
two storey Canadian house
in 1953
he was the first landlord
we ever knew
one by one he called his
siblings over to join him
and by 1963 he was tired
of hosting his extended clan
by the time my sister and i
snuck into his living room
to watch Bonanza on his
black and white television
he had almost forgotten
the reasons
he just very gently took our
small hands and led us out
closing his living room door
behind him and directed us
to the basement where our

rooms were
then he suggested that it
was my father's turn
to do the rest

my uncle Jake lives in
a very large house now
a very large house i have
never seen

# A Landscape

*[handwritten: excellent]*

she looks for the landscape
in the faces she loves

they have replaced the hills
the pastures of wild margherite
the fields of red poppies
where you and she promised
each other everything

*[handwritten: long for home — physically of Italy]*

the faces erase
the flat grey of this sky
they take these long
straight roads
and lead them
not to a piazza
but to open doors
where the laughter
inside keeps her safe
keeps her promising

she has parked her soul here
for what she believed was
a little while
and sometimes she cries
such hard tears
for the smell of new grass
after a rainfall
she cries such tears for
the light of fireflies
on an August night

*[handwritten: sense of betrayal]*

for a country that sent her away
without asking
and imprisoned forever
a child inside her heart
who keeps looking for landscapes
in the faces she loves

# St. Joseph's Girls

in 1967
dressed in my navy blue
wool uniform with a black
bow tie a blazer and sensible
oxfords i took the bus
from Lansdowne and St. Clair
to the Bloor subway station
i stood for the nine stops
to Sherbourne Avenue
i was a big girl
in grade nine
in the Centennial year
all on my own
crossing the big, big city
for my future

☆

St. Joseph's Commercial
was just a small school
nearly three hundred
immigrant girls
some light some dark
some big some small
and me, i was tall

☆

just across the street
from safe St. Joe's
was the Selby Hotel
seedy and sinful
where Hemingway
hung out in his days
when Toronto was a
hangout
we were warned about
the Selby Hotel
it was no place for
St. Joseph's girls
so we only had thoughts
about it

☆

Sister Laura Anne
taught us typing
like a religion

j-u-j space k-i-k space

the rhythm of her pointer
on the desk and ledge
our obedient fingers
hit the letters and the
thumbs caressed the space bars

she taught us Pitman shorthand
as if it were a secret language
that would reveal our lives
the lives of girls like me

to be shaped and molded
into fine secretaries

d-e-d space l-o-l space

but i could not write poetry
in Pitman shorthand
so i left

☆

the day Angela's sister died
all the girls of St. Joseph's
wore their neat bow ties
and their blue blazers buttoned
when they buried her
Angela's sister wore a
white long wedding gown
and you couldn't even tell
that she had been stabbed
seventeen times
that early morning
on Beaver Street
as she went off to work
pocket book in hand
smiling and free
her boyfriend decided her fate
and if she didn't want him
while she was living
he was going to have her dead

they dressed her in white
with a long thin veil over her eyes
her tiny hands were gloved

but she did not look like a bride
she just looked like a teenage girl
who thought once she might have
been in love

# Five Small Lives

she has dried the tomatoes
in the Canadian sun
it takes a little longer
but they are red and sweet
on the waiting tongue
she has blanched the green beans
bushels full
stored them in clear jars
with mint, garlic and olive oil
the house is giddy
with the wonderful smells
the mouth watering
ready for the tastes
only she can provide
she has labelled each jar
with her name
each letter perfectly
curled and slanted
in permanent black marker
her first and her last name
the one she learned to write
just to label her jars

☆

the sidewalks are made of cement
he understands cement
the way academics understand
the meaning of things beyond
what the words tell
he knows the amount of water

the necessary time for shaping
smoothing and setting
his hands are the size
of his work shoes
he cannot talk about much
blaming the language
the scarcity of time
but when he talks cement
what an articulate tongue

☆

Maria's bones are making her shorter
so she combs her hair
just a little bit higher
she is dreaming of freedom
from children and schools
dreaming of Paris or London
maybe a small villa in Tuscany
with roses and edible greens
Germaine Greer lives in Tuscany
perhaps they will exchange
gardening tips
but Maria is not a gardner
she is the eldest daughter
the unmarried one
the one who lives with her
mother

☆

the desk is still full
with things she belonged to
the pencil case with the
butterfly stickers

the pre-teen magazine
all the girls shared
the sharpened pencil crayons
neon markers and a word puzzle
that wasn't complete
she struggled with the english words
but they would soon come
the slightly scuffed running shoes
with the Barbie image on the side
were the new culture
she was learning to wear

the desk is still full
it will stay untouched
for the rest of the term
receiving the unspoken questions
of her classmates
why their friend
was thrown out of a balcony window
like a baseball
in the hands of a mad tortured man
who had one final statement to make

☆

Old man Joe
walks his dog
in the school yard
across the laneway
each night about 9:15
the signs are there
no dogs allowed
but he's learned to ignore
much more than signs

so he stands by the fence
and lets Carbone run free
then he whistles and the dog
comes running back
Joe's whistling is a musical tune

black as coal that dog is
black as night itself
unless the moon is full
you can only feel his movements

i have stopped on occasion
to exchange some words in Italian
his words are a thick dialect from a town
smaller than even he can remember
he calls me *Signora*
and there is respect in that word

i am a new immigrant in comparison
he has been here since 1949

where is the America of my grandfathers?
he asks
no longer here for sure
he answers
we left them the America
we made room, lots of room
for the ones who stayed behind
now they are comfortable
they sit in the sun
they collect the government cheques
they argue with their children
in a language they both understand

in this America
we must keep running
no time to sit in the sun
no time to walk the dog
in the daytime
but i am lucky
at least my dog understands
my whistle
*buona sera, Signora*
*buona sera*

# Notes on Aging

*I am a woman, and dusty, standing among new affairs.*
*I am a woman who hurries through my prayers.*
                                            Gwendolyn Brooks

i am middle aged now
something i thought
would only happen
to others
has happened to me

☆

i sometimes think
i have been old all my life
Italian women are born old
they carry the weight
right from the womb
old with fear
old with responsibility
the first beat of the heart
pounding out
fear fear fear
like the eleventh commandment

☆

lately it seems
all words are about
loss
always about leaving

☆

what to write
about my life
always in the past
the days become history
so quickly
i cannot write the future

☆

i am lost without dreams
when did they stop
such a dreamer i was
such fantasies
such possibilities
but all around me
there is pain
dreams have stopped
just like the candle light
at a quick breath
no warning
even my pen is heavy to lift

☆

i am looking for a reason
to write about snow
looking for a muse
in the cracks of my life
looking for a landscape
to tickle my heart
but i am sad
my steps are timid
in the winter night
awkward

how i miss running
how i miss the laughter
in my mother's house
where she lives alone
how i miss the length
of my hair
it's black sheen
faded
i miss my father's anger
how strange this
aging

☆

i will leave my poems
somewhere
in time they will be
stumbled upon
and my father's name
will live on
without sons

☆

i want to write
about my dying aunt
i hate the word
dying
she isn't dead yet
who am i to think
death must be the next
visitor
but the blood clots
are heavy and thick
like rocks

throughout her lungs
her right arm and leg
no longer move
her chest heaves
painfully
with each struggling breath
i bend to kiss her brow
her skin smells clean
sweet with talcum powder
i caress sparse white curls
little bundles of pure silk
i lift her still hand
to my lips
with a silent kiss
comes a prayer
asking for a miracle
all that is left
to believe in
but miracles don't happen
to old women
in Scarborough hospitals
in Canadian winters

☆

i am nothing
she is nothing
we are nothing
but a breath
a moment
a sunrise
a storm
a silence

☆

she asks me how i am
is my husband well
and my child, is she
growing strong and tall
go home, she tells me
the weather is bad
the road is long
between home and
here

☆

there is a slow tearing
in my heart
like a last love letter
another wound to heal
soon another gravestone
to visit
another voice in my life
silenced
another January
with its sharp icicles
plunged into my soul

☆

forty years
eighty years
a long time
a short time
when is death
less tragic

☆

it is life we lose
each time
and we are less
for it

☆

in my culture
middle-aged poets
are not highly regarded
unlike doctors or lawyers
and land developers
poets hold no position
you cannot measure
their worth
in real estate
my aunt
will not know
i write poems for her
life without metaphors
only the rhythm of
a broken language
she never acquired
thirty years spent
in airless factories
my dying aunt
will never hear my poems
but i know her life
helped me write them

☆

my heart is strong
my mother's lineage

in my father's family
the hearts were weak
my aunt hangs on
that muscle
broken over and over again
will not give up
women's hearts grow stronger
with each rupture
maybe
women's hearts never die
my aunt, my mother
my sister, my daughter
my nieces, me
one heart, forever stronger
infinite

# Dusty Women

because we are growing old
and we were not prepared
because we dreamed dreams
that were too big
and knew they would never happen
because we thought marrying for love
was nobler than marrying well
we are now sad and dusty with regret
we cannot blame anyone
the choices were ours
so we steal a Friday night
every other month of the year
and share it all
with bottles of Chardonnay
and nervous laughter
but together we make the anger subside
we have worked too hard, too long
we are tired
and a little empty with the weight of it all

maybe we never really knew what we wanted
maybe we have had it all along
and we still don't know it

# The Woman She Is

*For Dorothy Livesay*

the message is clear
each word precise
sculpted, carved
no unecessary stone
the rubble removed
beautiful birth
of language
poetry for the eyes
for the ears
for the red beating
heart

# First Born

mamma is the baby
in her family
three older sisters
and two older brothers

i am the first born

they are dying now
one by one
the giant uncles
with hands like shovels
the tough and gentle aunts
who fed me sausages
on fresh baked bread

mamma insists i accompany her
to each death
to each obligatory grave
so i put on my respectable
blue suit and i pin back my hair
i take mamma's arm and walk
with her to each casket
as she kneels i gently rest my hand
on her rounded shoulder
a position my father would have held

i help her to her feet
and grasp her elbow
as she bends to kiss the cold
pale brow

i hear the sounds
her knees make
and i hold her a little tighter

we walk the long line
exchanging hugs and
cool embraces
with each kiss a platitude
"the suffering is over"
"it was her turn"
"God called"
i bow my head with respect
i offer a smile

people whose faces are familiar
whose names i cannot recall
view me up and down
noting the changes
criticizing the red
of my nail polish
i continue to smile
and hold onto my mother
who has suddenly become
an old woman

i am the first born
who must accompany her
who must hold her arm steady
so she will not fall

# We Are the Good Children

we are the good children
so successful
we have built villas
for the surviving parent
landscaped the gardens
with exotic plants
added statues of angels
scattered them like trophies
of granite and marble
their wings entwined among
the thorns of well trimmed
rose bushes

we have smoothed down the
boccie courts
with fine red clay
lined them with comfortable benches
made of cedar and Canadian maple
the mandatory fountain in the middle
pissing away its wet song of nostalgia

we are the good children
so successful
we hold charity balls
where we dress up in Armani
sometimes Versace or Klein
the women perfectly waxed
the men perfectly groomed
we are beautiful
we are special

we parade ourselves
we celebrate our visibility

all this in honour of mothers and fathers
and of those who could not make themselves
comfortable in the hearts of children-in-law
for those who simply got too old to be of use

we are the good children
grown so sophisticated
so modern, so quickly
independent

but we have not forgotten
their sacrifices
we have not forgotten
our pockets full of money
the downpayments on our homes
the children they raised
while we were busy with the
adopted dream

so now we build villas
beautiful landscaped villas
without grandchildren
but we visit on Sundays
bringing fruit and photographs
we help feed the birds
for an hour or two
keeping an eye on the
slow moving
imported clock

40

# Good Friday, The Passion

the magnolia is resisting
the final winter slap
each year it struggles towards
another resurrection
each year i check the calendar
hoping for a premature re-birth

i want life again
in colour and perfume
i want the heat again in
white blinding sunshine
i want to stand at the corner
of Grace and Mansfield Avenue
on Good Friday
as the procession
makes its way unhurried
through the less catered streets
of my trendy neighbourhood

i want the sun to laugh at me
because the solemn faces
of my ancestors do not laugh
on such an occasion
they carry the cross
with reverence and apology

*generation & culture gap*

i am faithful
i attend each year
hoping i have grown
so sophisticated
i will finally carry
a video camera to record
the ethnic flavour
hoping i have grown
so liberated
i will sit at the Diplomatico Café
and laugh out loud
at the colourful spectacle
the way the new tourists
and temporary residents do
enjoying life as theater

but i am taken in each time
by the haunting voices
of women chanting the rosary
by the somber tune
of the one hymn i recognize
i am taken in each time
by the beautiful young girls
at their mother's arms
by the old men
who move like my grandfather
their slow steps
in tune with a trumpet

i am the lost daughter of nostalgia
but my heart is not saddened by this
and i will be here again
in the sunshine or in the rain
as Jesus falls one more time
in the streets of my neighbourhood
knowing that even i
will be somebody's history
somewhere along the line

# Ena and the Sleeping Giant

in the Havelock Hills
of Hawkes Bay
sleeps a giant
so the Maori legend tells
an enormous giant
spread out beneath
the long white cloud
of a country i fell in love with
when the man i love took my hand
and introduced me to the playgrounds
of his childhood landscapes
to a land of sea and hills
he brought me home
to a new family i belonged to instantly
to the Havelock garden
on Greenwood Road
where Ena sat each afternoon
on the wooden bench beneath
her open bedroom window
and with a voice that soothed
the weight of my journey
she shared the magic of
her New Zealand garden
the Latin and English name
of every flower and every plant
new and strange to my city girl heart
except for the rose and the passion flower
those i recognized from a time
in another garden
where my grandmother prayed on her knees

Ena offered me tea
by the persimmon tree
fat with orange fruit
an Autumn feast for birds
i felt embraced
Ena knew me by my foreign name
i knew her by her gentle touch
her elegant hands
her short bread cookies
on the silver tray
the arrangement of hydrangia
in the proper vase
sipping the sunlight slowly
like her five o'clock sherry

there is a giant asleep
in the hills of Havelock
in a land where my husband's
mother walks forever
among the gardens
that have no rival
where the rose and the passion fruit
grow beautiful and quiet

# I Wish I Were a Poet

i wish i were a poet
he said
so i could write about it

that your body became light
weightless
after the final turn
to its side
not by your own muscles
but by the hands of a stranger
paid to move you
that he would have wanted
to be there
to be those hands
to move your resigned flesh
to its comfortable side
to understand your last pain
your last pleasure
to understand the final breath
would he have seen
your soul rise from you
what shape
what intoxicating scent
it might bring
perhaps of your beloved roses
but he is here
a thousand miles away
in a pale green kitchen
thinking of you
as his tears mix

with strong black coffee
wishing he had
the power of metaphors
so he would not lose you

# Another Wedding

this church is ice cold
even in September
the flowers seem to shiver
in their delicate dress
of white satin ribbons
they are surrounded by
radiant candles
their blue flames
resisting the drafts
Joseph is standing
at the altar
his legs unsteady
he is waiting for the
Irish lady
he will make his wife
she will appear
through the great doors
of St. Francis
to the sounds of a harp
she rented for the occasion
Joseph's parents are here
hers are not
there are relatives from
the neighbourhood, friends
some from New York State
Joseph is a popular guy
it is a perfect month
for a wedding
the saints are polished
the carpet vaccumed

the priest is in a good mood
so we all comply and sing out loud
except for the old woman
by the far door
standing by the twin saints
Cosmus and Damian
she walks back and forth
pulling at her hair
lamenting without words
we all pretend she is not there
hiding our faces in our holy hands
mumbling some prayer by rote
moving to the sounds of bells
to the fragrance of incense
trying to play out this ritual
this sometime comedy
i want to understand

but i am still so primitive

# Some Grandmothers

sometimes
grandmothers are not
as strong as we think they are

sometimes little boys like Peter
who had no need for questions
but knew Grandma by the aromas
she so consistently provided
come home to a house without smells
and little boys like Peter
know instantly that something is not right
so little boys like Peter walk
the many steps into brand new rooms
of a suburban house
opening brand new doors to call out
Grandma's name
and then the final steps
into a basement Peter will never forget

sometimes
little boys like Peter
find Grandma hanging
by the strong home made ropes
of her own aprons

and among the piercing sound
of a little boy's screams
small trembling hands pull
on Grandma's feet
to get her down

then little boys like Peter
are left voiceless ← life Grandma
with a lifetime of unanswered
questions

# Two Fat Girls

in the 1970s
we walked St. Clair Avenue
from Dufferin to Lansdowne
as if it was our home town
as if we owned it
the wide Avenue with large sidewalks
spilling with other paesani who had
also claimed it theirs

grocery stores crammed with all
the delicacies from Sicily and Calabria
from Molise to Lazio
artichokes and eggplants like shiny trophies
on the sunny open market
Tre Mari Bakery where we stopped for *zeppole*
on the feast of St. Joseph
and that one treasured café
where we spent our street life
sipping cappuccino before they were  cool

maybe we were just two fat girls
maybe we were just two stupid girls
romantic and silly, just two young girls

i remember you wanted a husband
and i wanted just to be loved
and neither one of us knew
where to find what we were looking for
so we walked the Avenue
in our three inch heels

like models on a runway
with our skirts split at the back
our strong, young legs teasing
such innocence
you with your perfect breasts
and me the tall one
swinging our purses
to the rhythm of our hips
just past Tricolore Pool Hall
where the young immigrant studs
cigarettes in hand
whistled and lusted
"hey Susie baby, sleep with me
tonight,"
but we were just two fat girls
dark-haired and free
laughing out loud
as we paraded by
because we knew they
could only have us
with their eyes

# The Other Woman

when the Virgin Mary
is the other woman
you can kiss your
lover's heart  good-bye

when the Virgin Mary
is the ideal mother
you have lost the
argument with your son

when the Virgin Mary
is the ideal woman
no lipstick will ever be
the perfect shade

you are no competition

you are just a woman
with a mountain of faults
just flesh and blood
a woman whose hormones
are misunderstood
a woman too difficult
to console

so you can love them both
till your heart breaks
you can pray all the prayers
ever written
summon each blessed saint

for help and intervention
you can cry all the tears
of this evil world

you will never be salvation

you have bled in pain
lost your temper sometimes
even part of your mind
you have taken pills for comfort
smoked a cigarette or two
ironed enough shirts to dress the
planet

you are human
pure and simple

maybe it is time
you lifted yourself
from your bed of wounds
time you learned to love
yourself just a little

because the other woman
sometimes wins

Catholic Subordination
of women
– idealization
of virgin & virgin/mother
no one can
live up to that
ideal
natural progression
results in
disdain towards
women

# Leaving You

i leave you at l0:45
you are slipping
in and out of sleep
it's the morphine
because  you don't
like to sleep
that i remember

but i must leave you
at your most vulnerable
moment     the dark
the time you tell me
the demons come
but i am so tired
too tired to help you
fight them tonight

i am a little ashamed
to think of my own needs
my life, my job, my child
they are excuses
that help me move
from your bedside
they are the reasons
i step away like a thief
quietly in the night
hoping you will sleep through

but when i am in my own bed
i close my eyes

and sleep will not come
all i see in the darkened
screen of my lids
is your hands clutching
the hospital sheets
instead of my fingers

# The Setting

the chair
by the kitchen window
her body slumped
on it like dead weight
her head resting
in  the wrinkles
of her hand
her belly heaving
the pain of too
many dinners cooked
with love

his chair
by the kitchen table
his body rigid
against the wall
his eyes
on the flowers of
the large ceramic tiles
his hand caressing
the half glass of red wine

a morbid silence
is all these two
have shared for years

he has not known her breasts
the shape they have succumbed to
she has not felt his muscles
for a thousand years

they have made love
only in duty
right from the beginning

now they share the duty
of old age
the visits of respect
the obligatory appearance
arm in arm
at weddings and baptisms
awaiting, patiently
the one liberating
attendance at the first
death

*the life sentence of old word/cott.
trad. marriage*

# Ricordi, 1942

a pigtailed girl
shaped into brown rags
running in a ravished field
of limbs and bones
the red soil singing
a copper pail hanging
like a loose hand
from a broken wrist
running running
vomiting obscenities
and prayers
trying to reach a well
running running
under a raining thunder
of blind airplanes

# In London, Ontario, There Is a Cemetery

you refused to come
when your husband asked you
America was not your home
Pennsylvania was not your home
your husband would come and go
and he would father three of your
children before he decided
that you were more important than America
but your husband liked America
he would have made it work

then when you buried him
in the small plot in town
all your children were gone
to the other America
and Canada was not your home
but this time you had to come

and now your husband is there
and you are here
in a small plot beside strangers
in this soil so frozen and hard
this soil that never knew the
sweat from your resistant brow
never knew the strength of your arms

i bring you carnations in winter
and i ask forgiveness for our needs
hoping you understand the limbs that

*[handwritten annotation in right margin: "aspect of geog. as well as cultural alienation"]*

tremble above you
they are a little ashamed
a little puzzled by the irony
of life

# The Land

they sold my grandfather's land
less than an acre it was
with the old stone house still standing
five small rooms and a fireplace
a few scattered fruit trees
and some tall poplars
they cleared out the rosemary bush
for a cobblestone driveway
they sold my grandfather's land
because Canada is too far away
because all his children live here
because all his grandchildren
have names like Ashley and Glenn

they burned old furniture and photographs
burned grandma's old linen too
much too yellow to be of use
they cleaned house
to rest with old things of the past
they knocked down the barn
where Arduino and i milked the cow
the rabbit cages flattened
the pails and tools a heap of sculpture
after the flames died out

they sold it for a useless price
divided by five
because sibling cannot ever agree
because each one has a different memory

i look into my mother's face
and see the loss
"what have we done," she whimpers
i have learned to say the right words
the words that are needed

"it's only land, mamma, only land,"
i whisper with a very acrid tongue

She knows
even as she's
saying the words
that it's much
more than merely land

# Disability

disability is a dirty word

it takes a man's integrity
puts a number on it and files
it away on the third floor
on Avenue Road
in a three room office
with beige rugs and pastel prints
with *Time* and *Newsweek*
and a tall secretary
who lies about how busy
the doctor is

so you wait
until your one o'clock appointment
is honoured at two
and you are thankful

i am the interpreter
for a patient who does not
understand medical words
much less the paper work
or the attitude of the professional
doctor who takes the man's history
like so many paper formulas
but the doctor will never record
the history of immigrant pain
or of an accident that takes more
than the man's legs
but it takes his heart and soul

and when the medicine man
will not sign the papers
for a disability pension
he is almost surprised
at the lack of defiance
at the composure
and with his million dollar smile
he tells me
to take responsibility

# October 31

a young wife
opens a garage door
to find her husband
hanging by his leather belt
this image in her eyes  forever

and my friend is gone
on this ironic night
while my child runs excitedly
up and down stairs
in her pink fairy gown
gathering candies
like golden nuggets

my friend is gone
and i am numb with guilt
angry at my eyes
that could not see his pain
each morning on the Dufferin bus
our teacher's bags faithfully
by our sides rushing
to meet the bells
to be there for all the children
we were to enlighten
to prepare for life

suicide on Hallowe'en  night
such a statement for a good
catholic boy

# Eight Short Poems

*Ah, raccogliersi in sè, e pensare!*
*(Ah, to withdraw into myself and think!)*

Pier Paolo Pasolini

### one

if i had no memory
i could simply rest
i could find grace
in a new face

### two

to be alone in your own company
is to open in vain
nothing in your head
you are an orphan
you prepare your tea
and sandwich you idle
you exhaust yourself
with blame and excuses

### three

you are transparent
a beautiful void
so universal
you make me laugh
it is the unexpected
fulfillment you are
in your circle

the danger you consume
with pleasure
the position you hold
in this room without walls
where insects build kingdoms
do not breathe too close to me

four

it was easy then
the ideas were all about change
the thoughts free of punctuation
there was a new bloom
each time on the thorny bush
now there is endurance
entering is a struggle
and then you find you are
already dry in the center

five

i am tempted to move
to a house of my own
i pack my bags and each time
i prolong the departure
i cannot deny
i feel safe here

                    six

i am now a conformist
i have yielded
lost to my foolish and
youthful loves
life makes you tired


                            seven

if we are anything
we are brief
an orgasm at best
a blood clot at worst
a word
pulsating in time
very brief


                            eight

?

# The Caves of Pastena

just over the hill of Falvaterra
in the province of Lazio
you took me back to see
the mysterious caves
their obtrusive beauty
their darkness
you explained their history
and my fingers grazed
their rough and tangled mass
the sharp icicle points
like frozen rain
and then i remembered
my mother's memory
these caves
the war
they had once been a refuge
a haven for women and children
when the Germans came and took
everything, killed the pigs
and left nothing to eat but
the chestnuts and some potato
or some dismissed onion or two
it was here they waited
for the bombs to cease
for the war to end
it was here my aunt gave birth
to Anthony, on this muddy ground
stealing a glimpse at the sun
perhaps a longer look at the moon
until one spineless traitor

sold them all for a pack of cigarettes
to the Marrocchini who wanted women
my mother's memory
is everywhere in these rocks
in the dark heart of this cave
i must walk outside
i hope it's raining

# Some Women

they are the mavericks
daring to enter the room
the forbidden garden [uttering the unutterable]
where tresspassers
are condemned
but they persist
they scratch open the dark
and sometimes their heads rest
in open doors of gas ovens
sometimes they fill their glass
with the final taste of sweet poison
but they have walked in the garden
they have altered the shape of the room

they live

*[handwritten margin annotations: "uttering the unutterable" / "that Patriarcia identifies is little" / "there is doubt yet there still a detached admiration"]*

# I Cannot Write Love Poems
## Like Anne Sexton

there is a book on my bedside table
as permanent as the clock and lamp

Anne of the thousand wounds
and the full red lips
Anne of the dark brown eyes
of the sex and the suicide
Anne of the tortured bed
where she lies almost defeated
her heart in her open hands

that love should be so fragile
so beautiful and sad
that love should destroy so exquisitely

i cannot write love poems
like Anne Sexton
but there they are
treasured gifts left
to women like me
to women who need them

# Love Poem

he brings me tea in bed
he lets me sleep
until my body is ready
to stir
the light he allows in
is measured
he sits by my feet
and rests a hand
on my ankle
feeling my heartbeat
he loves me silently
undisturbing

this is something
i need to get used to

# The Collector

you have put me on a shelf
with all your other trophies
some dressed in a little more dust

in time i will be dusty too
in time all things will become trophies
and you will wonder why
you were so honoured

# For a Blue Lady

how many graves will
you dig for yourself

so you've been hurt
nothing new
nothing serious
just life

let the white ghosts lie
their cold fingers
have no place here
there is a new warmth
keeping the flesh together
measure your eyes
in his reflection

you are love now

you've written poems
from scattered fragments
this time the words come
easily like his smile
allow his gentleness
to fill you
the way Spring fills
all the holes Winter carves
so selfishly

# Femmina, 2000

my beautiful niece Luciana
has her mother's smile
her dark eyes slant sadly
the way my father's did
her long straight fingers
belong on the hands of an artist
but her hands do not work on
artistic things      not yet
her body is strong
erect and tall
her breasts round and shy
she is always dancing
cartwheeling in laughter
her thoughts are free
unbound by worry or time
her older brother calls her
*femmina*
it is the one word in Italian
he knows perfectly well
her brother is a bright young man
with a promising future
his respected Catholic Boys School
has given him awards and scholarships
he works hard, he studies hard
but his clean blue and white uniform
is often impeccably ironed by the
*femmina* of the house

# My Nephew

my brand new nephew and i
our noses glued to the new
bay window in the new house
in the new subdivision
watching the flashing light
on the Wonderland Mountain
my little Gatsby
mysterious little man
was there ever a time before you
before your smile
that floods my mother's eyes
before your needs
so selfish and immediate
before your arms so impulsive
your tiny hand on my shoulder
your cheek caressing mine
we watch the sky light up
with magic fireworks
like a storm of invading fireflies
your breath steady and warm
against my face
and i am prepared to give you anything
anything at all for the price of your smile

# We Are Just the Bricks

they will never talk about us
with any real respect
we are just the bricks
visible on the outside
inside they camouflage us
with fashionable prints
muted colours
trying to erase our texture
occasionally they will expose
a few of us
for a touch of esthetics

we are small sips
of required ethnic flavour    _trendiness_
we are never invited to dine
perhaps a wine and cheese
but we are never offered
the truly expensive wine

it has taken a while
but i have come to understand
so i often loiter on the outside
and i gaze at the bricks
i see the strength
the multitude of shades
how they hold up
against the wind and rain
the precision in which they lie
side by side, on top of each other
working together

but standing alone
and i think of my grandfather
and his wise and simple words
"remember, little girl,
you will know who you are
by the company you keep."

# Second Language

each language i speak
is a second language

there is a dialect
i understand my mother by

there are words i write
in English that my husband edits

there is a sound in my head
that sings my grandmother's songs

there is a language my heart speaks
that even i cannot translate

 but language is always an issue

and i want to give you a voice
such a voice to be envied
spoken without error
nouns and verbs in the proper place
they will be stunned by the strangeness
of it all, with the perfection of it all
your tongue unleashed like a wild
tango erotico

and you will give me your hands
with all their imperfections
open and waiting
i will read in them

the stories and poems
we will trade souls for a while
and again you will give me
the reason for listening
the reason for time and remembering
and i will tear a sheet
of clean fresh paper from my head
free to write you
in a language
that is first
second and last

a language our spirit
will understand

# Figli canadesi

chissà
se qualche volta
pensano a noi
due o tre generazioni
di noi
ormai ripiantati
cresciuti e sbocciati
in nuovi colori
tra i giardini di Toronto
Woodbridge e Bolton
tra i nuovi castelli
di King City

chissà
se qualche volta
pensano alle nostre ragioni
giuste ed ingiuste
al calcio in culo
chissà
se l' università
offrano dei corsi

chi siamo?
chi eravamo?

quanti figli cacciati
di casa
quanti orfani delusi

certi di noi

ancora cittadini
per memoria
per nostalgia
forse anche
per dispetto

# The Painter

*For Nick Palazzo*

you said you did not believe
in nationalities
"i am human, just human"
and then you went
and painted pain
in every language

i met you in a portrait
named Maria
something in her still eyes
and emptiness so full
her gnarled, misshapen hands
folded tightly on her lap
close to her belly
as if she were holding
back or in all the pain
of your dark secret world

Maria gave a face to my women
the women i write about
the ones who were formed
by nationalities

i learned that your name is Nick
such a strong name      direct
my heart was once broken
by a boy named Nick

86

# Someday I Will Read "Dover Beach"

Mr. Bowman wore a bow tie
for the three years i knew him
he had three suits
one gray, one green, one blue
the blue one he favoured
was thinning at the ass
by the time i graduated grade thirteen
but his shirts were always impeccable
i think he had the same love affair
with bleach that my mother has

Mr. Bowman was a proud English teacher
he was even more proud of his profound
knowledge of Chaucer, Milton and Donne
Mr. Bowman wanted all of us to be English too

One year i reluctantly showed him some poems
hoping he would choose one for our year book
and when he called me into his office
i had a grin you could stuff with a loaf of bread
and then with his perfect accent he inquired
"Giovanna, have you ever read 'Dover
        Beach'?"
and i, in my young, cocky semi-deliquent style,
answered, "no, sir, but i think i've heard of
        him"

Mr. Bowman was satisfied
he flashed his confident style
by pulling at his bow tie

"Giovanna," he said
"if you cannot write
like Matthew Arnold then
you really shouldn't write at all"

so i didn't
for a very long time

# Picasso had Paris

Picasso had Paris
and Gertrude Stein's
living room
where they all came
for scotch and conversation

Picasso had Paris
like a beautiful mistress
like a forgivable sin
he had the soul of his lover
and not just the sex
he had the night with all its
temptations
smoke filled cafés
where life clung and exploded
fireworks over the Seine

Pasolini had Rome
and its mysterious fountains
the dark side of the moon
behind the Cuppolas
he had the angels he loved
and the demons he fought
and Rome and the night
had his heart

i have Clinton and College
on a January night
with a skinny cappuccino
and a DuMaurier light

# One More Time

*For Arduino*

my love affair with Italy
is coming to an end
the passion is just a smoldering
a small spark that sometimes ignites
but quickly cools leaving only the memory

all affairs have their time

but on winter nights
when i fall into drawers
straightening the past
into neat little piles
i come across your photograph
your arm in mine
solid and secure
your short stained pants
your shy awkward smile
and i can almost taste
the figs you brought me
wrapped in their own
thick dark leaves
i can hear your voice
across the fields
clear as the doorbell
and that little boy
kiss you planted
forever in my heart

and sometimes i think
i would like to
fall in love again
one more time

# Ciao, Baby!

it was summer
the hills were a green
like moss gone sour
the sun hid behind them
like a child
between the safe folds
of a mother's skirt
the oak was full
like a giant umbrella
your bare feet dangled
among the fat, deep leaves
i looked up
you hit me with an acorn
turned your reckless hair
toward the sky
i called you again and again
begged you to come down
held out my hand
to trade one last walnut
one last shiny marble
you hit me again
and let me leave
with my hand still stretched
you let me leave
with the back of your head
on a great ship called Augustus
i left on a great adventure
without you
and you didn't even say
*Ciao, Baby!*

# L'ultima bambina

*For Francesca*

she is the last baby
i will fuss over
the last one to spoil
to love too much
the last one nonna
will walk to the park
with much slower steps
Francesca
with the chestnut eyes
the wise one with
the old woman smile
the one who sits
and listens to all our
conversations
with such deliberate patience
with such solid curiosity
and then off she goes
to search out the truth
in her little girl heart

Printed in September 1999 by

in Longueuil, Quebec